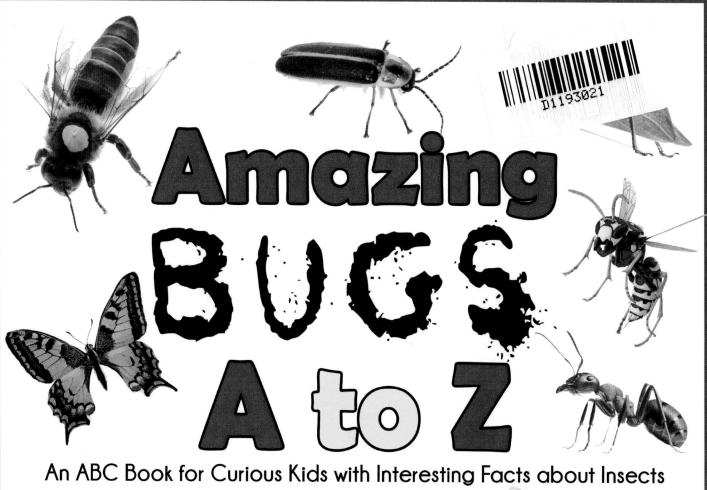

Amazing BUGS A to Z

An ABC Book for Curious Kids with Interesting Facts about Insects

Dylanna Press

A is for Ant

Did you know that ants can lift objects that are 10-50 times their weight? That's like you lifting a car! Ants are also great team players that work together to find food and build their homes, living in colonies of up to 500,000 ants. Next time you see ants outside, take a moment to appreciate their amazing strength and teamwork!

B is for Butterfly

Butterflies are like flying works of art! Butterflies can flap their colorful wings up to 20 times per second! They come in many bright colors and patterns, and some even have special designs that look like eyes to scare away predators. Did you know that butterflies eat with their feet? They use tiny taste buds to help them find the sweet nectar in flowers.

C  is for Cricket

Did you know that crickets communicate through song? They rub their wings together to make chirping sounds, kind of like a cricket orchestra. Male crickets do this to attract mates and scare off competition. Crickets are also great at jumping and can jump up to 30 times their own body length!

D is for Dragonfly

Did you know that dragonflies have been on Earth for more than 300 million years? They have been zipping around since the time of the dinosaurs! Dragonflies are known for their incredible speed and agility. They can fly forwards, backwards, up, down, and even hover in mid-air like a helicopter. This makes them excellent at catching mosquitoes – a single dragonfly can eat hundreds per day!

E is for Earwig

Earwigs might look a little scary with their long pincers, but they're actually quite harmless to humans! In fact, they mostly eat other insects and help keep our gardens healthy. Earwigs are also great recyclers – they eat decaying plants, fungi, and rotten fruit. Did you know that mother earwigs are great at taking care of their babies? She will watch over her eggs and babies until they're big enough to take care of themselves!

F is for Firefly

Fireflies are like tiny, glowing stars that come out at night to put on a light show! They use their light to communicate with each other and find a mate. Did you know that fireflies are actually beetles? They have special chemicals in their bodies that make them light up, kind of like a natural flashlight!

G is for Grasshopper

Grasshoppers are amazing! They can jump up to 20 times their own body length and also have wings that they can use to fly. Grasshoppers are skilled at camouflage and can change their color to blend in with their surroundings. Did you know that grasshoppers are herbivores and mostly eat plants?

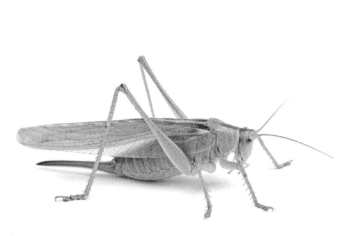

H    is for Honeybee

Honeybees are an incredible species! They live in colonies and have amazing social organization skills. They collect nectar from flowers and turn it into sweet, golden honey in their hives. Did you know that honeybees have a special dance to tell their friends where to find the best flowers? They wiggle and shake their bodies to share the location with the other bees!

I is for Inchworm

Inchworms are fascinating! They have a unique way of moving by arching and straightening their bodies, which makes them look like they are measuring the ground as they go. Did you know that inchworms are actually the larvae of moths and butterflies? They spin cocoons and transform into beautiful winged insects!

J    is for June Bug

June bugs are super cool! They have bright, shiny wings and love to fly around on warm summer nights. They like to munch on the leaves of trees and shrubs, so you can often find them around these plants. June bugs come in a variety of colors, from green to brown. Fun fact: June bugs are attracted to light. If you leave a porch light on at night, you might notice June bugs flying around it.

K is for Katydid

Katydids are amazing insects! Their green color and leaf-like shape make them blend in perfectly with the leaves of trees and plants, making them difficult for predators to spot. They make a unique noise that sounds like they are saying "katy-did" which is how they got their name. Try to spot these camouflaged critters in gardens and other outdoor spaces!

L  is for Ladybug

Ladybugs are small, colorful beetles that have vibrant red wings and distinctive black spots. Ladybugs are loved by gardeners because they love to eat pesky insects like aphids, which can harm plants. Did you know that ladybugs are also a symbol of good luck? Some people believe that if a ladybug lands on you, it means you'll have good fortune!

M is for Mosquito

Mosquitoes are like tiny vampires that love to suck blood! But did you know that only the female mosquitoes bite? They need blood to make eggs, while the males stick to eating nectar. Mosquitoes are also attracted to sweet scents and bright colors, so wearing dark, unscented clothing can help keep them away!

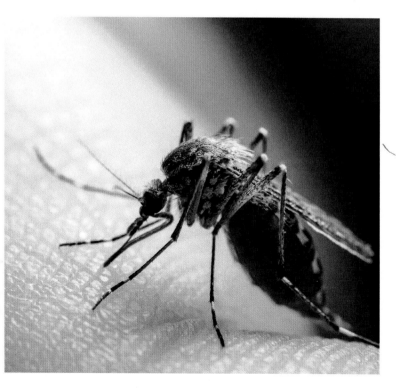

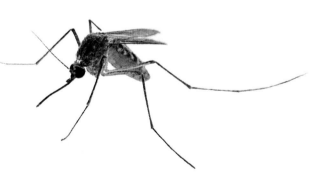

N is for Nymph

Nymphs are baby insects! They go through several stages of growth before becoming full-fledged adults. Nymphs often look like miniature versions of their adult form, but lack wings and can be less colorful than when they are fully grown. Nymph insects shed their outer layer (exoskeletons) several times as they grow and develop into adults.

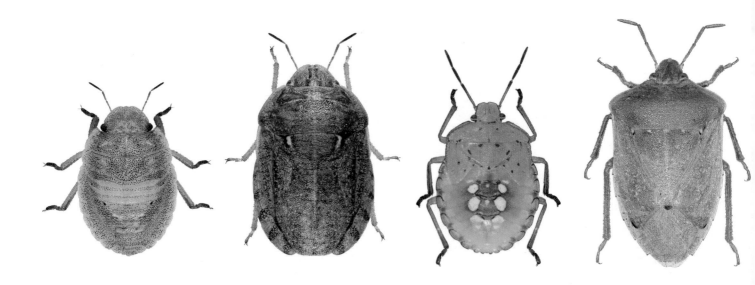

O  is for Owlfly

Owlflies come out at dawn and dusk to hunt other insects! These interesting creatures have large, owl-like eyes; long, thin bodies; and translucent wings. They hunt by using their long antennae to sense prey and then snatching them out of the air.

P   is for Praying Mantis

Praying mantises are fascinating insects known for their unique appearance and hunting skills. Long and slender with triangle-shaped heads, they use their large front legs to catch and hold their prey. Did you know that praying mantises are also masters of camouflage? They can blend in so well with their surroundings that they're almost invisible! Another fun fact about praying mantises is that they can turn their heads 180 degrees!

Q  is for Queen Bee

Queen bees are the rulers of the hive! They're the largest and most important bees in the colony, responsible for laying all the eggs and keeping the hive running smoothly. Did you know that queen bees can lay up to 2,000 eggs per day? That's like laying an egg every minute! Queens start out just like other bees, but they are fed a special diet of royal jelly that helps them to develop into queens. Queen bees live an average of 2-3 years.

R  is for Roach

Roaches are little survivors that can live almost any-where! They have been around for millions of years and can survive for weeks without food or water, and they can even survive for short periods of time without their heads! They are also fast-moving bugs that can run at speeds of up to 3 miles per hour.

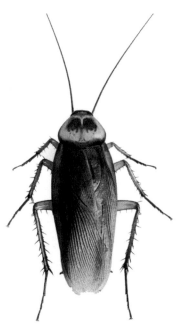

S    is for Stink Bug

Stink bugs are like little stink bombs that use their smell to defend themselves! When they feel threatened, they release a stinky odor that helps keep predators away. These shield-shaped bugs are found all over the world, and they are often seen crawling around on plants or flying through the air. Did you know that stink bugs are also great at camouflage? While many stink bugs are brown or gray, some species have bright colors and patterns on their bodies.

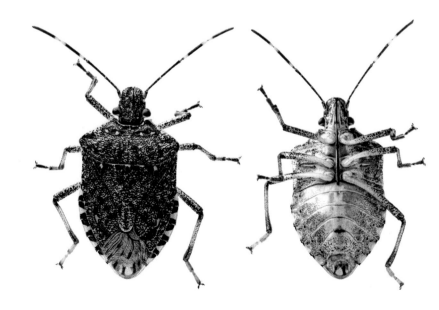

T is for Termite

Termites are like tiny builders that create incredible homes made of mud and wood! Often considered pests, they're important decomposers of wood, helping to recycle nutrients in the environment. They work together in large groups called colonies, and some termite colonies can have millions of members! Each termite has a specific role to play – there are workers, soldiers, and reproductive termites.

U is for Umbrella Wasp

Did you know that umbrella wasps build their nests upside-down to look like little umbrellas? Umbrella wasps, also called paper wasps, are often seen as scary or aggressive, but they play an important part in the ecosystem as pollinators, helping to spread pollen from plant to plant. They live in colonies with a queen wasp who is responsible for laying all the eggs in the colony, while the other wasps are divided into workers and soldiers that help to care for the young and defend the colony.

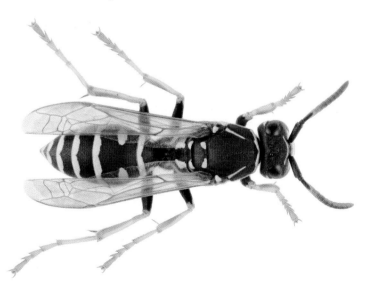

is for Velvet Ant

You may be surprised to learn that velvet ants aren't really ants at all! They're actually a type of wingless wasp. Males are brightly colored and covered in soft fur, while the females are black and yellow. They hunt other insects, like grasshoppers and beetles, by laying their eggs on them and using their venomous sting to paralyze them. Despite their painful sting, velvet ants are actually beneficial to humans because they help to control populations of other insects.

W is for Walking Stick

Did you know that walking stick insects look just like twigs? They are masters of disguise that blend in perfectly with their surroundings! Their long, thin bodies and stick-like appearance make them almost invisible to predators when they are resting on trees or bushes. They are also some of the biggest insects in the world, growing up to 12 inches long!

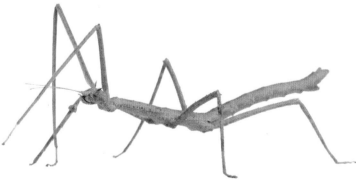

X is for Xylocopa

Xylocopa, also known as carpenter bees, are master builders of the insect world! They create nests in wood by drilling perfect holes using their strong jaws. These bees are among the largest bees in the world, with some species reaching up to 1 inch in length! Despite their large size, they are generally not aggressive towards humans and will only sting if they feel threatened.

Y  is for Yellowjacket

Yellowjackets are a type of wasp that have bright yellow and black stripes. They live in colonies and build their nests underground or in trees and are known for their aggressive behavior. Did you know that yellowjackets are also important predators of other insects? They catch flies, caterpillars, and other bugs to feed their babies and help keep the balance in the ecosystem. They also love sweets like plant nectar and fruits.

Z is for Zebra Butterfly

Zebra butterflies are beautiful insects that that are named for the distinctive black and white striped pattern on their wings. They are found in tropical and subtropical regions and can be seen flying in open fields, gardens, and forests. They are social butterflies, which means that they gather in groups of up to 50 to roost at night. They love to drink nectar from flowers, but unlike other butterflies they also eat pollen.